A COOKBOOK FOR A MAN WHO PROBABLY ONLY OWNS ONE SAUCEPAN

IDIOT-PROOF RECIPES

BADLY COOKED FOOD ON
BADLY DRAWN PLATE.
AVOID RESULTS LIKE THIS

LAGOON BOOKS

SITTING BULL WAS THOUGHT TO BE A
VERY POOR COOK AND IS MENTIONED
IN ANOTHER PART OF THIS BOOK

PUBLISHED IN 2000 BY
LAGOON BOOKS
PO BOX 311, KT2 5QW, UK
PO BOX 990676, BOSTON, MA 02199, USA
WWW.LAGOONGAMES.COM

ISBN: 1902813146

FIRST PUBLISHED IN AUSTRALIA IN 1998 BY
PAN MACMILLAN AUSTRALIA PTY LIMITED

COPYRIGHT © 1998 BILLY BLUE MERCHANDISING PTY LTD

RECIPES BY HELEN TRACEY AND LINDA KAPLAN

ADDITIONAL WRITING BY ROSS RENWICK

SUPERVISING CHEFS MATT BLUNDELL AND GAVIN CUMMINS
OF KENTRA DOUBLE BAY AUSTRALIA

MANAGING DIRECTOR AARON KAPLAN CREATIVE DIRECTOR ROSS RENWICK

PRINTED IN SINGAPORE

DEAR RECEIVER OF THIS BOOK.

THE WORDS ON THE
FRONT COVER
MAY BE AN
EMBARRASSMENT
TO YOU.

I HAVE PROVIDED
YOU WITH THREE
FAKE FRONT COVERS.

CHOOSE THE COVER
OF YOUR CHOICE
AND PASTE IT OVER
THE FRONT COVER.

Existentialism from Dostoyevsky to Sartre

Ziggy Zen

Matisse and the Poetry of Colour

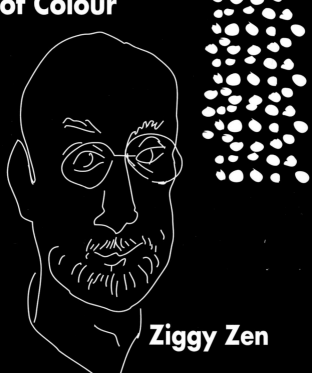

Ziggy Zen

Beethoven
and the
Quasi-Mathematical
Precision
of Tempo

Ziggy Zen

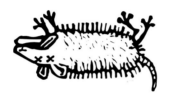

UNDER NO CIRCUMSTANCES USE ROADKILL
AS AN INGREDIENT

I
love
you...

but
it's
time
to say
goodbye

TO THE

WORLD OF COOKING

THE HEART AND SOUL OF COOKING

IN ANOTHER BOOK I MENTIONED A RECIPE THAT I GOT FROM ELVIS PRESLEY, NOW ALIVE AND LIVING UNDER THE NAME OF ELVIS MICHALOPOULOS. BUT IN FACT I GOT THE RECIPE FROM ANOTHER MAN WHO HAD BEEN CAPTURED BY ALIENS BUT TREATED KINDLY.

THEY TOOK HIM TO ANOTHER PLANET AND TAUGHT HIM EVERYTHING THERE WAS TO KNOW ABOUT MAKING STOCK, THE VERY HEART AND SOUL OF COOKING.

THE ALIENS SAID THAT THEIR MISSION WAS TO SPREAD GOOD STOCK RECIPES ACROSS THE 43 INHABITED PLANETS AND THAT STOCK MAKING ON EARTH, DESPITE THE CONSTANT POSING OF CHEFS, WAS THE WORST OF THE INHABITED PLANETS. WHAT THE ALIENS SAID ABOUT OUR ARCHITECTS AND POLITICIANS COULDN'T BE REPEATED HERE.

THE MAN SAID THAT HIS TRIP TO ANOTHER
PLANET COULD BE VERIFIED BECAUSE KEVIN
BACON WAS IN THE SAME CLASS. JUST ASK KEVIN,
HE SAID.

WELL, I'M NOT GOING TO GET ON A PLANE TO
HOLLYWOOD AND WALK UP TO KEVIN BLOODY
BACON IN THE STREET AND ASK HIM IF HE'S
RECENTLY BEEN LEARNING HOW TO MAKE GOOD
STOCK ON ANOTHER BLOODY PLANET.

ANYWAY, WHEN YOU'RE EATING THE RESULTS OF
THESE RECIPES LOOK AT THE NIGHT SKY.

ENJOY THE STOCK AND REMEMBER THAT
SOMEONE UP THERE'S EATING IT TOO.

THIS IS A BOWL,
FOOD GOES IN AT TOP

BOILED EGGS

START WITH EGGS AT ROOM TEMPERATURE. VERY COLD EGGS CRACK MORE EASILY IN BOILING WATER.

BRING WATER TO BOIL ON MODERATE HEAT, CAREFULLY LOWER EACH EGG INTO WATER ON A SPOON.

THIS LESSENS THE CHANCE OF THE SHELL CRACKING AND THE WHITE ESCAPING.

SIMMER FOR 5 MINUTES FOR SOFT-BOILED (8-10 FOR HARD-BOILED).

PLACE HARD-BOILED EGGS UNDER COLD RUNNING WATER AFTER COOKING; THIS PREVENTS THE EDGE OF THE YOLKS DARKENING.

TO PEEL, ROLL FIRST BETWEEN PALMS TO LOOSEN SHELL.

POACHED EGGS

HALF FILL FRYING PAN WITH WATER.

ADD 1 DESSERTSPOON VINEGAR OR STRAINED LEMON JUICE.

HEAT WATER TO JUST BOILING.

BREAK EGG INTO A SAUCER.

SLIDE GENTLY INTO WATER.

SIMMER GENTLY UNTIL WHITE IS SET, OR LONGER IF YOU WANT IT HARDER.

FRIED EGGS

HEAT 1 DESSERTSPOON OF OLIVE OIL IN FRYING PAN
ON MODERATE HEAT UNTIL VERY RUNNY AND HOT.

CRACK EGG INTO PAN (HIT THE MIDDLE OF THE EGG
GENTLY AGAINST THE EDGE OF THE STOVE OR PAN
UNTIL IT BREAKS).

FRY UNTIL IT REACHES DESIRED SOFTNESS OR
HARDNESS.

USE SPATULA TO ENCOURAGE OIL ONTO TOP OF EGG
TO COOK YOLK.

TURN IT OVER IF YOU LIKE IT THAT WAY.

I WAS ONCE IN THE ARMY, IN AN AMATEUR SORT OF
WAY CALLED NATIONAL SERVICE, AND LEARNED TO
SHOOT PEOPLE AND COOK SCRAMBLED EGGS.

SHOOTING PEOPLE IS LIKE MOST OTHER THINGS.
IF YOU'RE INTERESTED ENOUGH YOU CAN LEARN
TO DO IT. SCRAMBLED EGGS ARMY-STYLE IS
DIFFERENT.

YOU THROW A LARGE SACK OF POWDER INTO A HUGE
KEG AND THEN YOU HOSE IT WITH COLD WATER.
WITH A FEW STIRS IT BECOMES EGGS SCRAMBLED
ARMY COLD.

THIS IS ARMY BACK-TO-FRONT LANGUAGE. IT MEANS
COLD ARMY SCRAMBLED EGGS.

THEN YOU SERVE IT AND PEOPLE SAY, YOU DON'T
EXPECT ME TO EAT THIS SHIT, DO YOU?

IT'S LIKE THAT WHERE I LIVE, A SUBURB WITH EIGHT
CAFES. SEVEN OF THEM MAKE SCRAMBLED EGGS THAT
SHOULD BE USED AS A FILLER FOR BEANBAGS. THE
OTHER IS EVEN WORSE BUT MAKES A GOOD COFFEE.

Why do people open cafes when they can't make scrambled eggs or coffee?

Start a strict training regime. Make scrambled eggs eight times a day for a week. You'll be a star. But do me a favour. Don't open a cafe in my suburb.

Things are so bad out there you may as well eat at home.

SCRAMBLED EGGS

SERVES 4.

6 EGGS
6 TABLESPOONS MILK
1 DESSERTSPOON BUTTER
SALT AND PEPPER
PARSLEY TO GARNISH

LIGHTLY WHISK EGGS IN A BOWL.

ADD MILK, SALT AND PEPPER TO TASTE.

MELT BUTTER IN FRYING PAN.

POUR IN EGG MIXTURE.

COOK ON LOW HEAT UNTIL SET.

WITH WOODEN SPOON, DRAG MIXTURE AT EDGES TO CENTRE (THIS ALLOWS EVEN COOKING).

DO NOT STIR, THERE SHOULD BE LARGE CLOTS OF COOKED EGG.

SERVE IMMEDIATELY ON TOAST.

SPRINKLE WITH CHOPPED PARSLEY.

OPEN TO ENDLESS VARIATION:
  USE CREAM OR HALF CREAM FOR A MORE
  LUXURIOUS BREW.

  ADD CHOPPED SMOKED SALMON WHEN COOKED.

  ADD COOKED BACON, MUSHROOMS, CORN.

  FRESH HERBS WILL ENHANCE THE LOOK AND THE
  FLAVOUR E.G., BASIL, OREGANO, PARSLEY, THYME.

OMELETTE

SERVES 1.

2 EGGS
1 TABLESPOON MILK
SALT AND PEPPER
2 TEASPOONS BUTTER
PARSLEY TO GARNISH

LIGHTLY BEAT EGGS AND MILK TOGETHER.

SEASON.

HEAT PAN AND ADD BUTTER (YOU CAN USE OIL,
OR A MIXTURE OF BOTH).

WHEN BUTTER IS FOAMING (NOT BROWN),
ADD EGG MIX.

COOK ON MODERATE HEAT.

LIFT MIXTURE WITH SPATULA SO UNCOOKED EGG
RUNS UNDERNEATH.

COOK UNTIL EGG IS SET AND GOLDEN.

LOOSEN FROM PAN WITH SPATULA, FOLD IN HALF.

SERVE GARNISHED WITH PARSLEY.

VARIATION: BEFORE FOLDING, YOU MAY ADD SMOKED OR CANNED SALMON, HERBS, SPINACH (CHOPPED AND COOKED), CREAMED CORN, CHOPPED TOMATOES, CHOPPED ASPARAGUS, COOKED MUSHROOMS, PRAWNS ETC.

GAZPACHO

A MEXICAN CHILLED SOUP.

SERVES 4-6.

500g/4-5 CUPS LEFTOVER MIXED SALAD, INCLUDING LETTUCE, TOMATO, CUCUMBER, CAPSICUM, ONION, SALAD DRESSING

2 400g/14oz CAN OF TOMATOES

SALT AND FRESHLY GROUND PEPPER

PUT SALAD IN FOOD PROCESSOR AND BLEND.

ADD TOMATOES AND BLEND UNTIL SMOOTH.

SEASON TO TASTE.

SPRINKLE WITH FRESH HERBS, SUCH AS CHOPPED MINT, BASIL OR PARSLEY AND ICE CUBES.

GRILLED TOMATO AND PESTO

A SNACK OR AN IMPRESSIVE SIDE DISH.
SERVES 4.

4 RIPE TOMATOES

PINCH OF SUGAR

**3 TABLESPOONS PESTO SAUCE
(FROM DELI)**

BLACK PEPPER

BALSAMIC VINEGAR

PREHEAT GRILL.

SLICE TOMATOES IN HALF.

PLACE ON OILED GRILL.

SPRINKLE SMALL AMOUNT OF SUGAR ON EACH.

GRILL TOMATOES UNTIL SLIGHTLY BLACKENED
AND SOFT.

REMOVE FROM GRILL, DRIZZLE WITH
BALSAMIC VINEGAR.

PUT A TEASPOONFUL OF PESTO ON EACH TOMATO.

GRIND FRESH BLACK PEPPER OVER EACH.

SERVE HOT.

MEATBALLS

1kg/2lb MINCE — BEEF, VEAL OR PORK
1 PACKET FRENCH ONION SOUP MIX
SOUR CREAM TO MIX (2 OR 3 TABLESPOONS APPROXIMATELY)
1 TABLESPOON CHOPPED PARSLEY

PREHEAT OVEN TO 160°C/300°F/GAS MARK 2.

MIX ALL INGREDIENTS TOGETHER IN BOWL, DON'T MAKE IT TOO SLOPPY. IT HAS TO HOLD TOGETHER.

ROLL INTO BALLS, ABOUT 1 DESSERTSPOON PER BALL.

PLACE ON HEATED BAKING TRAY AND BAKE 15 MINUTES.

SERVE AS SNACK FOOD.

DIP IN CHILLI SAUCE IF YOU LIKE.

THE SPOON IS FOR
STICKING INTO FOOD

PUMPKIN AND COCONUT SOUP

SERVED COLD AND CAN BE MADE AHEAD.

1 DESSERTSPOON BUTTER OR OLIVE OIL

1 MEDIUM ONION, FINELY CHOPPED

1 CLOVE GARLIC, CRUSHED

500g/1lb PUMPKIN, PEELED AND CHOPPED INTO 2.5cm CUBES

1 LITRE/1 3/4 PINTS VEGETABLE STOCK (OR MAKE SOME WITH A CUBE AND 1 LITRE WATER)

150g/5oz CAN COCONUT MILK

COCONUT TO GARNISH, SHREDDED

IN LARGE PAN, HEAT BUTTER, ONION AND GARLIC AND COOK 2 MINUTES.

STIR IN PUMPKIN AND STOCK AND SIMMER UNTIL PUMPKIN IS TENDER (ABOUT 20 MINUTES).

ADD COCONUT MILK AND STIR.

REMOVE FROM HEAT AND COOL.

CAN BE MADE TWO DAYS AHEAD (KEEP COVERED IN REFRIGERATOR).

SERVE COLD, SPRINKLED WITH SHREDDED COCONUT.

THE PAN IS FOR STICKING FOOD INTO

LEEK AND PEAR SOUP

WHEN YOU WANT THEM TO THINK YOU'RE
AN EXPERIENCED CHEF.

SERVES 6.

75g/^{1}/$_3$ CUP BUTTER

**200g/7oz LEEKS, WELL WASHED
    AND CHOPPED**

4 PEARS, PEELED, CORED AND SLICED

1 ^{1}/$_2$ LITRES/2^1/$_2$ PINTS CHICKEN STOCK

SALT AND PEPPER

SPRIGS OF FRESH DILL

MELT BUTTER IN LARGE SAUCEPAN.

ADD LEEKS AND PEARS.

SAUTE (FRY GENTLY) OVER MODERATE HEAT
FOR 10 MINUTES.

ADD STOCK AND SIMMER, COVERED,
FOR 30 MINUTES.

ADD SALT AND PEPPER TO TASTE.

SERVE WITH A SPRIG OF DILL FLOATING IN THE MIDDLE.

THE FORK IS FOR
STICKING INTO FOOD

VEGETABLE SOUP

2 MEDIUM ONIONS

1 MEDIUM CARROT

1 STALK CELERY

2 MEDIUM POTATOES

1 CLOVE GARLIC, CHOPPED

2 VEGETABLE STOCK CUBES

2 TABLESPOONS OLIVE OIL

**ASSORTMENT OF VEGETABLES
OF YOUR CHOICE**

DOLLOP OF TOMATO SAUCE

SOY SAUCE

SALT AND PEPPER

ROUGHLY CHOP VEGETABLES.

SAUTE THE ONIONS IN OLIVE OIL UNTIL SOFT.

ADD CARROT, POTATOES, CELERY AND GARLIC,
KEEP COOKING.

ADD ENOUGH WATER TO COVER VEGETABLES
AND COOK, STIRRING FOR 2 MINUTES.

ADD STOCK CUBES, REST OF VEGETABLES, TOMATO
SAUCE, SOY SAUCE AND SALT AND PEPPER.

ADJUST WATER LEVEL TO COVER VEGETABLES.

SIMMER FOR 1 HOUR OR UNTIL VEGETABLES
ARE COOKED.

ADD CHOPPED PARSLEY AS YOU SERVE.

SERVE WITH WARM CRUSTY BREAD ROLLS.

VINAIGRETTE

ALSO KNOWN AS FRENCH DRESSING, IT'S THE OILY – LOOKING ONE WHICH NEEDS TO BE SHAKEN BEFORE USE (IT SEPARATES IN THE JAR). THERE IS MUCH DISCUSSION AMONGST AFICIONADOS ABOUT THE CORRECT RATIO OF OIL TO VINEGAR, BUT ALL THAT MEANS IS IT'S IMPOSSIBLE TO GO WRONG.

180ml/$^3/_4$ CUP OLIVE OIL

60ml/$^1/_4$ CUP CIDER VINEGAR (OR LEMON JUICE)

$^1/_4$ TEASPOON DRY MUSTARD POWDER

1 CLOVE GARLIC, CRUSHED

1 TABLESPOON CHOPPED CHIVES OR FRESH BASIL OR LEMON THYME

PUT ALL INGREDIENTS IN A SCREW-TOP JAR.

SHAKE.

MAKES 250ml/1 CUP.

VARIATION: ADD 2 TEASPOONS WHOLE-GRAIN MUSTARD.

MAYONNAISE IN A BLENDER

THIS IS A CREAMY-LOOKING ONE.

2 EGGS
$1/_2$ TABLESPOON VINEGAR
$1/_2$ TABLESPOON LEMON JUICE
$1/_2$ TEASPOON DRY MUSTARD POWDER
$1/_4$ TEASPOON SALT
PINCH CAYENNE PEPPER
250ml/1 CUP OLIVE OIL

PUT EGGS, LEMON JUICE, VINEGAR, MUSTARD, SALT AND CAYENNE PEPPER INTO BLENDER AND TURN ON.

CONTINUE BLENDING WHILE ADDING OIL IN A THIN STEADY STREAM, BLENDING UNTIL THICK.

IF TOO THICK, ADD EXTRA VINEGAR OR WATER.

MAKES 300g/1$1/_2$ CUPS.

ANCIENT BLENDER

MICROWAVE HOLLANDAISE SAUCE

45g/2oz BUTTER

2 EGG YOLKS

4 TABLESPOONS MILK

2 TEASPOONS LEMON JUICE

$\frac{1}{2}$ TEASPOON DRY MUSTARD POWDER

PINCH OF PAPRIKA

PLACE BUTTER IN BOWL. MICROWAVE ON 100% POWER TO MELT (ABOUT 1 MINUTE).

WHISK IN REMAINING INGREDIENTS.

MICROWAVE ON 50% POWER UNTIL THICKENED, (ABOUT 2 OR 3 MINUTES), WHISKING EVERY MINUTE.

CAN BE POURED OVER MANY COOKED VEGETABLES — TRY ASPARAGUS, GREEN BEANS, CAULIFLOWER, SPINACH, CARROTS, OR ON...

EGGS FLORENTINE

COOK 1 BOX OF FROZEN SPINACH, FOLLOWING INSTRUCTIONS ON PACKET.

POACH 2 EGGS (SEE PAGE 15).

PLACE EGGS ON SPINACH.

POUR HOLLANDAISE SAUCE OVER.

GARNISH WITH PARSLEY.

TOMATO SAUCE

SERVES A MULTITUDE OF PURPOSES — OVER PASTA, CHICKEN FILLETS, FISH, PIZZA; MAKES WHATEVER IT IS FABULOUS.

4 OR 5 MEDIUM TOMATOES
$1/2$ BROWN ONION
1 STICK CELERY
1 SPRIG OF PARSLEY
1 CARROT
10 LEAVES BASIL
1 CLOVE GARLIC
FRESHLY GROUND BLACK PEPPER

CUT VEGETABLES INTO SMALL PIECES.

PUT IN SAUCEPAN WITH HERBS, GARLIC AND PEPPER.

COOK ON MEDIUM HEAT FOR 20-30 MINUTES.

PUSH SAUCE THROUGH STRAINER WITH WOODEN SPOON.

CHECK SEASONING AND ADD MORE HERBS, PEPPER TO TASTE.

KEEPS FOR 2 OR 3 DAYS IN FRIDGE (OR CAN BE FROZEN).

VARIATION: ADD CHILLI POWDER.

WHITE SAUCE

2 TABLESPOONS BUTTER
2 TABLESPOONS PLAIN FLOUR
250ml/1 CUP MILK
SALT AND PEPPER
PINCH OF NUTMEG

MELT BUTTER IN SAUCEPAN OVER MODERATE HEAT.

STIR IN FLOUR AND COOK UNTIL FROTHY.

GRADUALLY ADD MILK, STIRRING CONSTANTLY.

STIR OVER MEDIUM HEAT, MAKING SURE THE SPOON TRAVELS TO ALL PARTS OF THE BOTTOM OF THE SAUCEPAN.

KEEP STIRRING UNTIL SAUCE BOILS AND THICKENS, TURN DOWN TO A SIMMER.

COOK FOR A FURTHER 2 MINUTES.

SEASON WITH SALT, PEPPER AND NUTMEG TO TASTE.

THE SECRET: STEADY CONSTANT STIRRING.

POTATOES

THE EASIEST FOOD IN THE WORLD TO COOK AND SOME WOULD SAY THE MOST SATISFYING.

POTATOES STAND WELL ALONE, OR SUPPORT ALMOST ANY OTHER MEAL.

THEY ALSO COOK IN MANY WAYS.

EVERYONE CAN BE AN EXPERT ON POTATOES.

ROAST POTATOES

ALLOW 3-4 PIECES PER PERSON

WASH POTATOES.

PEEL IF DESIRED.

CUT INTO EVEN-SIZED PIECES AND RINSE.

COVER BOTTOM OF BAKING DISH WITH 1mm OF OLIVE OIL.

HEAT BAKING DISH IN A 220°C/425°F/GAS MARK 7 OVEN.

DRY POTATOES AND PLACE IN HEATED BAKING DISH, BASTE WITH THE HOT OIL (THIS SEALS THE CRUST IMMEDIATELY).

TURN POTATOES EVERY 20 MINUTES.

COOK FOR ABOUT 1 HOUR UNTIL GOLDEN
ON ALL SIDES.

SERVE WITH SALAD, MEATS, FISH, STEAMED
VEGETABLES.

HINTS: YOU CAN SPEED UP THE PROCESS BY GENTLY
FRYING POTATOES IN PAN ON TOP OF STOVE FOR 10
MINUTES BEFORE THEY GO IN THE OVEN.

IF YOU ROUGHEN THE SURFACE OF THE POTATOES
WITH A FORK, IT HELPS FORM A CRUNCHY CRUST.

VARIATION: YOU CAN ROAST PUMPKIN, PARSNIP,
SWEET POTATO, BEETROOT, CARROT, ONION.

YOU COULD ADD SMALL ONIONS OR CLOVES OF
GARLIC (PEELED).

OR THROW IN A FEW SPRIGS OF ROSEMARY.

MASHED POTATOES

WASH POTATOES (1 OR 2 PER PERSON) AND PEEL IF DESIRED.

CUT INTO EVEN SIZES.

BOIL IN ENOUGH WATER TO COVER FOR 15-20 MINUTES.

DRAIN OFF WATER COMPLETELY.

ADD A KNOB OF BUTTER AND 2 TABLESPOONS OF CREAM OR MILK PER 500g/1lb OF POTATOES.

MASH WITH MASHER UNTIL SMOOTH AND CREAMY.

ADD SALT AND PEPPER TO TASTE.

PARSLEY NEW POTATOES

CHOOSE SMALL, WHITE SCRUBBED POTATOES.

ALLOW 3 OR 4 PER PERSON.

WASH THE POTATOES, CHOPPING OFF ANY PIECES YOU WOULDN'T WANT TO EAT.

PUT IN SAUCEPAN AND JUST COVER WITH COLD WATER. ADD SPRIG OF MINT, 1 TABLESPOON OF SALT.

BRING TO BOIL AND COOK UNTIL TENDER — ABOUT 15 MINUTES.

DRAIN WELL.

SERVE WITH MELTED BUTTER AND CHOPPED PARSLEY.

SEASON TO TASTE.

PORK

RICE
BOILED RICE

50g/¼ CUP UNCOOKED RICE WILL GIVE 200g/1 CUP COOKED RICE.

LONG-GRAIN RICE IS USUALLY USED FOR SAVOURY DISHES.

200g/1 CUP WHITE RICE

500ml/2 CUPS WATER

PINCH OF SALT IF DESIRED

PUT RICE AND WATER IN SAUCEPAN.

BOIL GENTLY, UNCOVERED, UNTIL SOFT (APPROXIMATELY 20 MINUTES).

TASTE A FEW GRAINS TO TEST.

BEEF

ABSORPTION METHOD

200g/1 CUP BROWN LONG-GRAIN RICE
500ml/2 CUPS WATER
SALT (OPTIONAL)

PUT RICE AND WATER IN SAUCEPAN.

BRING TO BOIL OVER MODERATE HEAT.

COVER TIGHTLY.

COOK ON VERY LOW HEAT FOR 25 MINUTES OR UNTIL COOKED.

FISH

COOKING PASTA

IN A LARGE SAUCEPAN, BOIL A LOT OF WATER – PASTA LIKES TO MOVE AROUND WHILE IT IS COOKING. USE $1/2$ TEASPOON OF SALT TO 1 LITRE/ $1^3/_4$ PINTS OF WATER.

HOW MUCH PASTA? ABOUT 50g/2oz PER PERSON. (READ HOW MUCH THE PACKET WEIGHS.)

ADD PASTA SLOWLY, SWIRLING IT AROUND SO IT DOESN'T STICK.

DON'T PUT A LID ON IT, KEEP IT BOILING FAST.

IT WILL TAKE BETWEEN 5 AND 10 MINUTES TO COOK. THE TIME DEPENDS ON THE TYPE OF PASTA. (READ THE PACKET AGAIN.)

PASTA IS COOKED WHEN IT IS SOFT YET FIRM TO THE BITE *(AL DENTE)*. YOU CAN PULL A COUPLE OF STRANDS OUT WITH A FORK TO TASTE.

DRAIN WELL. IF YOU LIKE, TOSS THROUGH A TEASPOON OF OLIVE OIL TO STOP THE PASTA FROM STICKING TOGETHER, UNLESS YOU ARE GOING TO ADD A SAUCE TO IT.

ROUGH PASTA COOKING GUIDE:

SPAGHETTI: 7–10 MINUTES

VERMICELLI: 4–6 MINUTES

SPIRALS: 6–9 MINUTES

LASAGNE: 5–8 MINUTES

WHOLEMEAL LASAGNE: 8-10 MINUTES

(WHOLEMEAL PASTA WILL ALWAYS TAKE A BIT LONGER)

PASTA SAUCES

AS EASY OR AS COMPLEX AS YOU WANT.

THE SIMPLEST IS A SPOONFUL OF BUTTER AND A SPOONFUL OF CHOPPED PARSLEY. OR YOU CAN TRY SOME OF THE FOLLOWING.

A CAN OF TUNA AND SOME FRIED, CHOPPED GARLIC AND CHILLI.

A CAN OF PASTA SAUCE FROM THE SUPERMARKET.

STEAMED VEGETABLES.

STEAMED ASPARAGUS AND SLIVERS OF SMOKED SALMON AND HALVED CHERRY TOMATOES.

PESTO (BUY IT FROM YOUR DELI).

GRATED TASTY CHEESE.

THE REMAINS OF LAST NIGHT'S TAKEAWAY.

GARLIC BREAD

BUY A LONG BREAD STICK OR 2.

MAKE A MIXTURE OF BUTTER AND FINELY CHOPPED GARLIC IN A BOWL, THEN ADD CHOPPED PARSLEY OR OTHER HERBS.

CUT BREAD INTO 5CM SLICES OR WHATEVER YOU WANT, BUT KEEP THE SHAPE OF THE LOAF.

LIBERALLY SPREAD THE BUTTER/GARLIC MIXTURE BETWEEN EACH SLICE.

TRANSFER 30cm LENGTHS OF BREAD TO FOIL AND WRAP LOOSELY.

BAKE IN OVEN YOU HAVE PREHEATED TO 200°C/400°F/GAS MARK 6 FOR 10 MINUTES.

OPEN OUT FOIL AND RETURN TO OVEN FOR 2 MINUTES.

VARIATION WITH PITA BREAD:

SPLIT PITA BREAD IN HALF.

SPREAD INNER SIDE WITH BUTTER AND GARLIC.

ADD SESAME SEEDS OR GRATED CHEESE IF YOU LIKE. CUT IN SLICES OR WEDGES OR WHATEVER.

COOK AT 190°C/375°F/GAS MARK 5 FOR 10 MINUTES OR UNTIL GOLDEN.

STUFFED VEGETABLES

REALLY EASY.

TOMATOES

CUT TOPS OFF TOMATOES.

SCOOP OUT PULP.

REMOVE CORE AND RESERVE REST OF PULP.

COMBINE TOMATO PULP WITH BREADCRUMBS, GRATED CHEESE AND BASIL.

BAKE AT 180°C/350°F/GAS MARK 4 FOR 10 MINUTES.

OR

COMBINE TOMATO PULP WITH COOKED RICE, CHILLI AND CHOPPED SPRING ONIONS.

SPOON FILLING INTO TOMATOES.

TOP WITH EXTRA GRATED CHEESE.

BAKE AT 180°C/350°F/GAS MARK 4 FOR 10 MINUTES.

LAMB

MUSHROOMS

REMOVE STEMS.

CHOP STEMS AND FRY IN BUTTER WITH CHOPPED ONION AND CHOPPED BACON.

ADD A HANDFUL OF BREADCRUMBS, 1 TABLESPOON CHOPPED PARSLEY AND SEASONING.

MIX.

BRUSH OUTSIDE OF MUSHROOM CAPS WITH MELTED BUTTER.

GRILL THIS SIDE FOR 2 MINUTES.

TURN OVER AND SPOON BREADCRUMB MIXTURE INTO HOLLOW.

GRILL UNTIL GOLDEN.

VARIATION: CAPSICUM, COURGETTES, PUMPKINS GO WELL TOO.

YOU CAN BE CREATIVE WITH FILLINGS.

YOU CAN STUFF EGGS TOO: ADD MAYONNAISE AND MUSTARD TO THE YOLKS AND MASH IT UP.

STIR-FRIES

CUT ANY VEGETABLES INTO BITE-SIZE PIECES (ROUNDS, STICKS OR DIAGONALS).

HEAT SMALL AMOUNT OF OIL IN A FRYING PAN OR WOK.

ADD VEGETABLES THAT NEED THE LONGEST COOKING – ONION, POTATO, CARROT.

STIR FREQUENTLY, PARTIALLY COOKING, AVOID STICKING.

ADD REMAINING VEGETABLES ACCORDING TO COOKING TIMES (SEE PAGES 50-51).

KEEP STIRRING (ADD A DASH OF SOY SAUCE IF YOU LIKE).

COOK UNTIL TENDER BUT NOT OVERDONE.

SERVE WITH RICE AND BAKED POTATOES.

VARIATION: ADD COCONUT MILK TOWARDS END OF COOKING.

ADD UP TO 1 DESSERTSPOON LEMON JUICE AT END OF COOKING AND STIR IN.

ADD CHOPPED PINEAPPLE.

ADD CHILLI SAUCE.

ADD A HANDFUL OF NUTS (CASHEWS ARE GOOD).

GREEN SALAD

SURE, PEOPLE GET VERY INVENTIVE WITH SALADS, BUT THERE IS NOTHING WRONG WITH THE PURIST APPROACH.

WASH A FEW HANDFULS OF SALAD LEAVES.

ADD A FEW VISUAL ELEMENTS – ALL OR ANY OF THE FOLLOWING:

CHERRY TOMATOES, SPRING ONIONS, FRESH HERBS, BASIL, MINT, CHIVES, GRATED CARROT, CAPSICUM, FENNEL, CORN SLICED OFF THE COB, OLIVES, FETTA CHEESE.

ARRANGE TO YOUR HEART'S CONTENT IN YOUR DESIGNATED SALAD BOWL.

POUR OVER MAYONNAISE, VINAIGRETTE OR PLAIN LEMON JUICE.

OR

COMBINE JUST A FEW OF INGREDIENTS FOR A SIMPLE EFFECT.

SAY, TOMATO, CHOPPED BASIL AND OLIVE OIL. GRATED CARROT AND COCONUT. COOKED RICE, CAPSICUM, OLIVES AND VINAIGRETTE. SPINACH, MUSHROOMS AND FLAKED ALMONDS. VINAIGRETTE, APPLE, CELERY, WALNUT PIECES AND MAYONNAISE.

HOW TO COOK A LEG OF LAMB

2kg/4lb LEG OF LAMB

125ml/¹/₂ CUP OLIVE OIL

**3 CLOVES GARLIC, PEELED AND
  CUT IN SLIVERS**

SPRIGS OF ROSEMARY

SELECT A LEG WITH LITTLE FAT.

INSERT SLIVERS OF GARLIC INTO LEG.

PLACE FAT SIDE UP ON RACK OF BAKING TRAY.
ADD SPRIGS OF ROSEMARY.

ROAST IN PREHEATED OVEN AT 160°C/300°F/
GAS MARK 2.

FOR MEDIUM, COOK 20-25 MINUTES PER 500g/1lb
PLUS 20 MINUTES.

FOR WELL DONE, COOK 25-30 MINUTES PER 500g/1lb
PLUS 20 MINUTES.

INSERT SKEWER; IF JUICES ARE VERY BLOODY, COOK
LONGER AND CHECK AGAIN.

SERVE WITH MINT SAUCE, NEW POTATOES AND
STEAMED GREEN VEGETABLES.

AND MAYBE...

GRAVY

POUR FAT FROM ROASTING DISH, LEAVING 1 TABLESPOON.

SPRINKLE $1^1/_2$ TABLESPOONS OF FLOUR INTO PAN (TWICE THAT FOR THICK GRAVY).

BROWN SLIGHTLY.

SLOWLY ADD 250ml/1 CUP OF WATER OR VEGETABLE WATER, STIRRING CONSTANTLY.

ADD A STOCK CUBE FOR EXTRA FLAVOUR.

STIR UNTIL BOILING, MAKING SURE ALL OF THE BOTTOM OF THE PAN GETS STIRRED. IF IT GOES LUMPY, POUR IT THROUGH A SIEVE.

SEASON.

POUR OVER CARVED LAMB.

HOW TO COOK AARON'S INTERNATIONALLY RECOGNISED CHICKEN

1 ½ kg/3lb CHICKEN, MAYBE CORN-FED

PREHEAT OVEN TO 200°C/400°F/GAS MARK 6.

IN A SAUCEPAN, ASSEMBLE:

1 FULL TEASPOON SALT

¼ TEASPOON WHITE PEPPER

A PINCH OF PAPRIKA

4 CHICKEN STOCK CUBES

4 BEEF STOCK CUBES

1 TEASPOON HONEY

1 TEASPOON GRATED GINGER

1 HEAPED TEASPOON GRATED GREEN APPLE

1 HEAPED TEASPOON MARMITE (YEAST EXTRACT)

375ml/1 ½ CUPS WATER

ADD 1 LARGE ONION, DICED AND FRIED IN OIL.

SEPARATELY FRY 2 CHOPPED CLOVES OF GARLIC IN OLIVE OIL AND DRAIN.

ADD TO SAUCE AND HEAT, STIRRING UNTIL BLENDED.

POUR OVER CHICKEN IN A BAKING PAN.

COVER WITH FOIL.

COOK FOR 30 MINUTES.

REMOVE FOIL.

BASTE WITH JUICES EVERY 15 MINUTES.

AFTER ANOTHER 30 MINUTES, TURN CHICKEN OVER.

KEEP BASTING.

COOK FOR A TOTAL OF $1^1/_2$ HOURS.

REMOVE FROM OVEN.

LOOSELY REWRAP IN FOIL AND COVER WITH TEA TOWELS.

LEAVE COVERED FOR A COUPLE OF HOURS.

SERVE.

NOT A CHICKEN

CARPETBAG SAUSAGES

SAUSAGES, AS MANY AS YOU NEED
BOTTLE/S OF OYSTERS
TOMATO SAUCE OR WORCESTERSHIRE SAUCE

BARBECUE THE SAUSAGES.

OPEN THE OYSTERS.

SLIT THE SAUSAGES DOWN THE MIDDLE.

STUFF THEM FULL OF OYSTERS.

ADD WHICHEVER SAUCE YOU LIKE, OR BOTH.

SERVE THEM WITH SALAD AND CRUSTY BREAD ROLLS.

POLITICALLY INCORRECT RECIPE

FISH PIE

1 OR 2 CANS TUNA (DEPENDING ON HOW MANY PEOPLE ARE EATING)

1 CAPSICUM, CHOPPED

1 CAN CORN KERNELS

3 EGGS, HARD-BOILED

1 ONION, CHOPPED

DASH OF OLIVE OIL

WHITE SAUCE (SEE PAGE 29) WITH 100g/1 CUP GRATED CHEESE ADDED AND STIRRED IN

HANDFUL OF BREADCRUMBS

KNOB OF BUTTER

BROWN ONION IN OLIVE OIL.

PUT TUNA, CORN, CAPSICUM, ONIONS AND CHOPPED HARD-BOILED EGGS IN AN OVENPROOF DISH.

SEASON.

COVER WITH WHITE CHEESE SAUCE.

SPRINKLE WITH BREADCRUMBS AND DOT WITH BUTTER.

BAKE AT 200°C/400°F/GAS MARK 6 FOR 30 MINUTES OR UNTIL BREADCRUMBS ARE CRISP.

HOW TO COOK VEGETABLES

CUT OFF WILTED OR DISCOLOURED PARTS.

CHOP VEGS INTO SAME-SIZE PIECES FOR
EVEN COOKING.

COOKING TIMES MAY VARY DEPENDING ON THE
SIZE OF PIECES.

WHEN ALMOST COOKED, TEST WITH A FORK OR THE TIP
OF A SHARP KNIFE, EVERYONE HAS DIFFERENT
PREFERENCES FOR TENDERNESS OR CRUNCHINESS, E.G.,
FOR CARROTS, CAULIFLOWER AND BEANS.

BUT DO MAKE SURE STARCHY VEGS ARE COOKED
RIGHT THROUGH (POTATO AND ITS RELATIVES).

AND DON'T OVERCOOK GREEN VEGS, THEY WILL
BECOME FLACCID.

ASPARAGUS – BOIL 5-10 MINUTES, LYING SPEARS
DOWN IN WATER.

AUBERGINE/EGGPLANT – SLICE, SPRINKLE WITH
SALT, LEAVE 30 MINUTES, RINSE AND PAT DRY.

DIP SLICES IN FLOUR, BRUSH WITH OLIVE OIL AND BAKE
FOR 30 MINUTES IN A MODERATE OVEN.

BEANS – (GREEN) REMOVE STRING IF NECESSARY,
SLICE DIAGONALLY OR LEAVE WHOLE, STEAM 5-10
MINUTES.

BROCCOLI – CUT INTO SPRIGS, STEAM 10 MINUTES.

CABBAGE – CHOP COARSELY, STIR-FRY IN 1 TABLESPOON BUTTER OR OIL.

CAPSICUM – REMOVE SEEDS, SLICE, BRUSH WITH OLIVE OIL. GRILL SLOWLY UNTIL SOFT.

CARROT – PEEL AND SLICE, STEAM 10 MINUTES, OR ADD TO STIR-FRY, OR GRATE INTO SALAD.

CAULIFLOWER – CUT INTO SPRIGS, STEAM 10 MINUTES, SPRINKLE WITH CHEESE AND BROWN UNDER GRILL.

CORN – REMOVE HUSKS, THEN SILK (RUB WITH WET HANDS) AND BOIL FOR 10 MINUTES.

PARSNIP – PEEL AND CUT LENGTHWISE, ROAST AT 180°C/350°F/GAS MARK 4 FOR 45 MINUTES OR SO.

POTATOES – SEE THEIR OWN SECTION (SEE PAGES 30-33), OR SCRUB AND BOIL 20 MINUTES.

PUMPKIN – CUT UP INTO WEDGES. STEAM 20 MINUTES OR ROAST SAME AS PARSNIP.

SILVERBEET – WASH, CHOP FINELY, ADD 3-4 TABLESPOONS WATER, BOIL 5-10 MINUTES.

SWEET POTATO – SCRUB, SLICE AND STEAM 10 MINUTES, OR ROAST ABOUT 45 MINUTES.

YAMS – SCRUB, BOIL 10 MINUTES OR BAKE 40 MINUTES.

TO BAKE OR ROAST – HEAT YOUR OVEN TO 180°C/350°F/GAS MARK 4.

DESSERTS

NEARLY EVERYONE LOVES DESSERT, AND SIMPLE DESSERTS ARE FABULOUS.

CONSIDER THESE:

A PLATE OF SLICED FRUIT — AND DON'T FORGET FIGS! OR PINK PAPAYA DRIZZLED WITH LIME JUICE.

A CHEESE AND NUT PLATTER.

FRUIT SALAD OF CANNED BOYSENBERRIES, SLICED BANANAS AND LYCHEES.

ADD MARSHMALLOWS.

MANDARIN AND PINEAPPLE SEGMENTS WITH SHREDDED COCONUT AND SOUR CREAM.

FROZEN GRAPES.

WRAP A BANANA IN FOIL WITH THE JUICE OF A LEMON AND A SPOONFUL OF HONEY. BAKE IN A PREHEATED OVEN AT 180°C/350°F/GAS MARK 4 UNTIL TENDER. SERVE WITH YOGHURT AND NUTS.

SPECIAL STRAWBERRIES

PUT ENOUGH WASHED STRAWBERRIES IN ONE BOWL.

PUT SOUR CREAM IN ANOTHER BOWL.

AND BROWN SUGAR IN ANOTHER.

GIVE EVERYONE A LITTLE FORK.

TELL THEM TO DIP EACH STRAWBERRY IN SOUR CREAM
THEN IN BROWN SUGAR.

THEN TELL THEM TO EAT IT.

FRUIT SUNDAE

IN A CHAMPAGNE GLASS, LAYER RIPE PEELED STONE
FRUITS, FRESH PUREED BERRIES AND YOGHURT.

SPRINKLE WITH FLAKED ALMONDS.

BREAD AND BUTTER PUDDING

SERVES 4-6.

4 SLICES TOAST BREAD, CUT IN TRIANGLES

2 TABLESPOONS SULTANAS OR RAISINS

40g/$\frac{1}{4}$ CUP BROWN SUGAR

1 TEASPOON GRATED LEMON RIND

3 EGGS

500g/2 CUPS MILK

MAKE LAYERS OF BREAD, SULTANAS, SUGAR AND LEMON RIND IN OVENPROOF DISH.

IN A BOWL, BEAT EGGS AND MILK TOGETHER.

POUR OVER THE LAYERS OF BREAD.

LEAVE IT TO ABSORB FOR 10 MINUTES.

BAKE AT 180°C/350°F/GAS MARK 4 FOR $\frac{1}{2}$ HOUR OR UNTIL SET AND GOLDEN.

ICE-CREAM

COMMERCIAL ICE-CREAM CAN BE
DRESSED UP ENDLESSLY.

FIRST, SOFTEN IT OUT OF THE FREEZER FOR 15
MINUTES OR SO (DEPENDING ON THE TEMPERATURE).

ADD ANY OF THE FOLLOWING, EITHER BY FOLDING
THROUGH SO THAT IT MAKES SWIRLS, OR BY MIXING IN
COMPLETELY (YOUR EYE WILL TELL YOU).

CHOPPED GLACE FRUITS, SAY, GINGER OR CHERRIES,
OR FRUIT CAKE MIX.

ANY FRUIT PUREE; MANGO IS GREAT, BUT SO
ARE OTHERS.

CHOCOLATE FLAKES.

SLIVERS OF MANGO, STRAWBERRY OR NECTARINE.

PASSIONFRUIT PULP.

COCONUT.

MARSHMALLOWS.

THEN PUT IT BACK IN THE FREEZER FOR AN HOUR OR
UNTIL REFROZEN.

FUDGE CAKE

1 BLOCK OF CHOCOLATE, MILK OR DARK,
1 PACKET PLAIN BISCUITS
1 CAN CONDENSED MILK

MELT CHOCOLATE IN SAUCEPAN.

DO THIS SLOWLY, CHOCOLATE CAN BURN.

THE BEST WAY IS TO SIT YOUR SAUCEPAN IN ANOTHER BIGGER SAUCEPAN WHICH HAS SOME WATER IN IT. THEN MELT IT.

ADD CONDENSED MILK AND CRUSHED BISCUITS.

TO CRUSH THEM, YOU COULD PUT THEM IN A PLASTIC OR PAPER BAG, COVER THEM WITH A CLOTH, AND HIT WITH A SOLID OBJECT OF YOUR CHOOSING.

PRESS INTO SHALLOW SANDWICH TIN OR SIMILAR.

LEAVE FOR 24 HOURS.

CUT INTO SMALL PIECES.

A LITTLE IMAGINATION
AND A FEW MOMENTS OF YOUR TIME.

MAKE YOUR FUDGE CAKE LIKE A FAMOUS BUILDING
AND IMPRESS YOUR FRIENDS

JAM PASTRIES

1 PACKET PUFF PASTRY (THE ALREADY ROLLED-OUT ONE)

1 JAR RASPBERRY JAM, OR USE YOUR FAVOURITE

PREHEAT OVEN TO 180°C/350°F/GAS MARK 4.

SPRINKLE FLOUR ONTO A CHOPPING BOARD.

PUT A SLICE OF PASTRY ON IT AND CUT INTO PIECES.

OBLONGS ARE GOOD, BUT TETRAHEDRONS ARE BETTER OR STARS OR FISH.

BUT DON'T MAKE THEM TOO BIG.

PUT A SMEAR OF JAM ON EACH ONE.

PUT ON HOT OVEN TRAY.

BAKE 10 MINUTES OR UNTIL GOLDEN AND RISEN.

SERVE WITH THICK CREAM, OR CUSTARD, FRUIT PUREES OR ICE-CREAM AND FRUIT SALAD, OR BE INVENTIVE.

JAM

HELP WITH WEIGHTS AND MEASURES

1 CUP = 250ML

1 TABLESPOON = 15ML

1 DESSERTSPOON = 10ML

1 TEASPOON = 5ML

$\frac{1}{2}$ TEASPOON = 2.5ML

BUTTER — 2 TABLESPOONS = 30G

CHEESE, GRATED, FIRMLY PACKED — 1 CUP = 100G

FLOUR — 1 CUP = 125G

MILK — 1 CUP = 250ML

RICE — 2 TABLESPOONS = 25G

WHITE SUGAR — 2 TABLESPOONS = 30G

(1 CUP = 200G)

BROWN SUGAR — 1 CUP, LOOSELY PACKED = 150G

NOTE: 1 CUP MEANS 1 TEACUP, NOT A COFFEE MUG.

STORING FOOD

COVER FOOD IN THE FRIDGE; IT STOPS DRYING OUT AND TAINTING OF OTHER FOOD.

STORE GREEN AND SOFT VEGETABLES AND SOFT OR RIPE FRUIT IN FRIDGE IN THE CRISPER SECTION.

STORE POTATOES IN COOL DARK PLACE. LIGHT TURNS THEM GREEN, AND GREEN POTATOES CAN POISON YOU (SO DON'T EAT THEM!).

RIPEN AVOCADOS AND BANANAS IN BROWN PAPER BAGS IN A COOL SPOT (NOT IN THE FRIDGE, THEY WILL GO SOFT AND SWEATY).

MAKING THE BEST OF SHOPPING

REMEMBER THAT MANY THINGS ARE AVAILABLE THESE DAYS READY MADE.

SPEND HALF AN HOUR IN YOUR DELI JUST CHECKING OUT THE CONTENTS OF THE SHELVES.

CHECK PASTA SAUCES FOR EXAMPLE. ALL YOU DO IS BOIL UP THE PASTA AND ADD THE SAUCE.

DON'T BE AFRAID TO TAKE HOME SOMETHING MADE BY ANOTHER AND MAKE IT YOUR OWN WITH JUDICIOUS ADDITIONS.

DON'T FORGET SUPERMARKETS ARE CATERING FOR EASY MEALS TOO.

EVEN TAKEAWAYS CAN BE MADE TO LOOK AS THOUGH YOU HAVE PERSONALLY PREPARED THEM.

YOU CAN ADD STEAMED VEGETABLES TO JUST ABOUT ANYTHING (MAKES IT GO FURTHER TOO).

YOU CAN ADD CREATIVE GARNISHES.

AND SERVE IT ALL UP IN BEAUTIFUL DISHES.

YOU CAN COOK YOUR OWN RICE (SEE PAGE 34) ON THE DAY.

ALWAYS MAKE A LIST OF WHAT YOU NEED, AND THEN TAKE IT WITH YOU.

IF YOU ARE GOING TO FOLLOW A RECIPE, MAKE SURE THAT YOU HAVE ALL THE INGREDIENTS AND PUT THEM ON YOUR LIST IF YOU HAVEN'T.

TRY TO GO SHOPPING WHEN THE SHOPS AREN'T TOO BUSY, UNLESS YOU LIKE STANDING IN QUEUES.

KITCHEN COOKING EQUIPMENT – WHAT DO YOU NEED?

A COUPLE OF WOODEN SPOONS, DIFFERENT SIZES ARE GOOD.

A CAN OPENER

VARIOUS SHARP KNIVES, FOR MEAT, FOR VEGETABLES, FOR BREAD.

A CHOPPING BOARD OR TWO, MAYBE ONE LARGER, ONE SMALLER.

A COLANDER FOR DRAINING THINGS.

A FRYING PAN

ABOUT 3 SAUCEPANS, SAY, SMALL, MEDIUM AND LARGE. IT'S WORTH BUYING QUALITY, THEN EVERYTHING WON'T STICK.

A STEAMER

A SPATULA FOR LIFTING THINGS OUT OF FRYING PANS.

TONGS FOR HANDLING PASTA OR TURNING THINGS OVER OR FIDDLING WITH VERY HOT THINGS.

SOUP LADLE, MASHER AND SCISSORS

AN EGG BEATER

OVENPROOF DISHES, SIZES TO SUIT YOUR HABITS.

A MEASURING JUG

A GRATER

A POTATO PEELER

OPTIONAL:

A BLENDER, A JUICER, A WOK, A SANDWICH MAKER,
A MICROWAVE OVEN, A GARLIC CRUSHER.

HOW TO APPROACH A RECIPE

ALWAYS READ ALL OF THE RECIPE BEFORE YOU START.

ALWAYS CHECK YOU HAVE ALL THE INGREDIENTS
BEFORE YOU START.

PREHEAT OVEN BEFORE STARTING FOOD PREPARATION.

ALLOW HALF AN HOUR, ALTHOUGH THIS VARIES
GREATLY BETWEEN OVENS (GAS IS ALWAYS QUICKER).

THE HOTTEST PART OF THE OVEN IS THE TOP.

UNLESS OTHERWISE STATED, RECIPES USUALLY
MEAN THE MIDDLE OF THE OVEN.

ALL OVENS ARE VARIABLE, SO BE PREPARED TO ADJUST
COOKING TIMES A LITTLE.

RECIPES ARE ONLY A GUIDE, DON'T BE AFRAID
TO EXPERIMENT.

TAKE IT SLOWLY AND FOLLOW THE INSTRUCTIONS.

OTHER BOOKS IN THE ZIGGY ZEN SERIES:

How to drink wine out of fish heads while cooking lobster in a volkswagon hub cap

ISBN: 1902813138

The mafia just moved in next door and they're dropping by for dinner cookbook

ISBN: 1902813154

How to become a dinner party legend and avoid crippling psychological damage

ISBN: 1902813162

For more titles, visit
Lagoon Books website at
www.lagoongames.com